The Teacher

By Jenny Giles
Photographs by Lindsay Edwards

I am at school
with my friends.

We are going
to see our teacher.

We go into the classroom,
and our teacher smiles at us.

We help her with the books.

In the morning,

we have our news time.

Our teacher talks to us,

and we talk to her.

She writes a story with us,

and we read it with her.

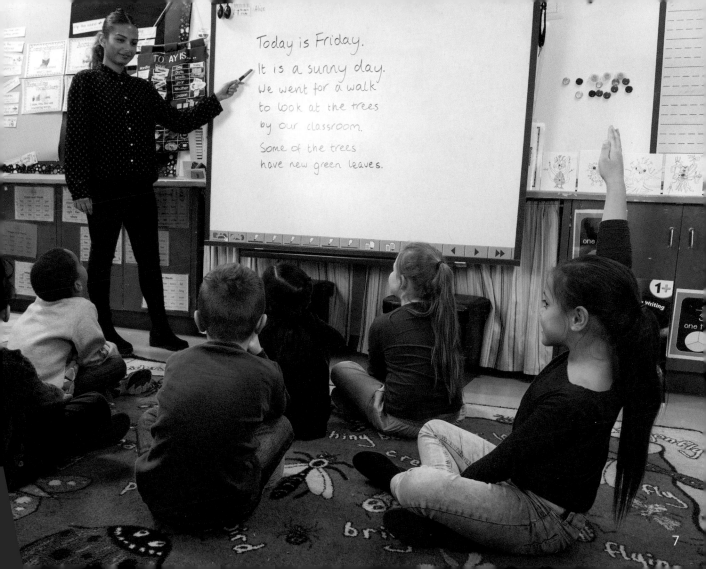

Today is Friday.
It is a sunny day.
We went for a walk
to look at the trees
by our classroom.
Some of the trees
have new green leaves.

I read my book to the teacher.

The teacher reads a story to us.

At playtime,

we go outside.

We run and play games,

and our teacher looks after us.

After play,

we run into the classroom.

Our teacher is not pleased,

and she stops us.

She says that someone will get hurt

if we run inside.

She makes us walk.

We do math at school.

The teacher helps us

with our work.

I am good at math.

After school, Mom comes to get me.

I wave to my teacher, and I go home.